Extreme Wakeboarding Moves

By A. R. Schaefer

Consultant:
Scott N. Atkinson
Director of Communications
USA Water Ski

CAPSTONE
HIGH-INTEREST
BOOKS

an imprint of Capstone Press
Mankato, Minnesota

Capstone High-Interest Books are published by Capstone Press
151 Good Counsel Drive, P.O. Box 669, Mankato, Minnesota 56002
http://www.capstone-press.com

Library of Congress Cataloging-in-Publication Data
Schaefer, A. R. (Adam Richard), 1976-
   Extreme wakeboarding moves / by A.R. Schaefer.
   p. cm.—(Behind the moves)
   Includes bibliographical references (p. 31) and index.
   Contents: Extreme wakeboarding—Basic moves—Extreme tricks—Safety.
   ISBN 0-7368-1515-5 (hardcover)
   1. Wakeboarding—Juvenile literature. 2. Extreme sports—Juvenile literature.
[1. Wakeboarding. 2. Extreme sports.] I. Title. II. Title: Extreme wake boarding
moves. III. Series.
GV840.W34S32 2003
797.3'2—dc21   2002010812

Summary: Discusses the sport of extreme wakeboarding, including the moves
involved in the sport.

Editorial Credits
Angela Kaelberer, editor; Karen Risch, product planning editor; Kia Adams,
   series designer; Gene Bentdahl and Molly Nei, book designers; Jo Miller,
   photo researcher

Photo Credits
Corbis/Rick Doyle, 4, 10
Getty Images/Adam Pretty, cover, 8, 21; Chris McGrath, 4 (inset), 7, 10 (inset),
   18; Bryan Mitchell, 12, 14; Darren England, 13, 26; Mike Hewitt, 16 (top);
   Robert Cianflone, 29
islerphoto/Mike Isler, 22, 23
SportsChrome-USA, 16 (bottom), 18 (inset), 26 (inset)
USA Water Ski/Scott Atkinson, 20, 25

1 2 3 4 5 6 08 07 06 05 04 03

Table of Contents

Tony Finn invented the skurfer.

Learn about:

- **The first wakeboards**
- **Wakeboarding basics**
- **Equipment**

Chapter One

Extreme Wakeboarding

In 1985, California surfer Tony Finn had an idea. Finn wanted a surfboard he could use on a lake. He designed a small surfboard that could be pulled with a rope behind a boat. Finn called his invention a Skurfer. As a boat speeds through water, it leaves a trail of ripples called a wake. Skurfers rode the wake like surfboards ride waves.

Finn's invention was not perfect. Riders often fell off Skurfers, so Finn added foot straps to the boards. Riders still had a hard time balancing on the long, narrow boards. Skurfers also floated on top of the water. Riders could not easily get on the boards.

Wakeboard Improvements

In 1989, Herb O'Brien changed the Skurfer. His design allowed riders to easily get on the board. O'Brien called his new board the Hyperlite. Many people say the Hyperlite was the first wakeboard.

By the early 1990s, companies had made other improvements to wakeboards. They added small fins to the nose and tail of the boards. The fins helped riders steer. Most wakeboards have two fins, but some have as many as six.

Wakeboard companies also added bindings to the boards. Bindings look like shoes or boots. The bindings hold riders' feet onto the boards.

Wakeboarding ropes are attached to a handle. Riders hold onto the handle as the boat pulls the board.

Wakeboarding Basics

Riders stand sideways on the board. The side closest to the rider's heel is called the heelside edge. The side closest to the toes is the toeside edge. Riders either stand regular foot or goofy foot. Regular-foot position is left foot in front. Riders who stand goofy foot have the right foot in front.

Riders use their feet and weight to control the board's direction. When riders push down with their toes, the board goes one way. When riders push down with their heels, the board goes in the opposite direction.

Bindings hold riders' feet on the boards.

Wakeboarding is part of the X Games.

Extreme Wakeboarding

Wakeboard riders began performing tricks after the sport became popular. Riders performed some tricks on the water's surface. They performed other tricks called aerials in the air.

In 1992, riders gathered in Orlando, Florida, for the first professional extreme wakeboard competition. This competition later became known as the Pro Wakeboard Tour. In 1996, wakeboarders first competed in the X Games. Today, wakeboarders also compete in the Gravity Games, the Vans Triple Crown of Wakeboarding, and the Wakeboard World Cup.

Professional wakeboarders compete on courses made up of sliders and ramps set into the water. Sliders look like railings. They sometimes are made of plastic pipes and floating blocks. Sliders and ramps allow riders to do jumps and high aerial tricks. Riders receive scores from the judges based on the number and difficulty of their tricks.

Learn about:

- **Catching air**
- **Rolls and flips**
- **Spins and grabs**

Chapter Two

Basic Moves

Some basic wakeboarding tricks come from skateboarding, snowboarding, and other extreme sports. Wakeboarders also invent their own tricks.

Catching Air

Riders must get in the air to do many tricks. Most riders use the wake to catch air. First, the rider moves sideways toward the wake. Riders call this action "cutting in." As the board rides up the wake, riders push down with both feet as they straighten their legs. The board then pops into the air.

Riders can cut in or out of the wake either toeside or heelside. Riders who cut in toeside have their backs to the boat. Riders who cut in heelside face the boat.

Rolls and Flips

Riders use the wake to perform rolls. A wakeboarder cuts the board toeside across the water into the wake. When the board hits the wake, it pops into the air. Riders then push their weight forward and flip their legs and board over their head. Riders look like they are doing a somersault in the air. Riders land facing the same direction they were as they started the trick.

A roll looks like a somersault.

A flip begins much like a roll. But the rider cuts heelside into the wake. As the board pops, riders kick their legs out and over their head one at a time. A flip looks like a cartwheel in the air.

A flip looks like a cartwheel in the air.

Spins

Wakeboarders do two types of spins. During surface spins, the rider turns the board while it is in the water. Other spins are performed in the air.

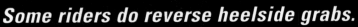
Some riders do reverse heelside grabs.

Spins are measured in degrees. A half-spin is 180 degrees, so the trick is called a 180. A full spin is a 360. A 720 includes two full spins. Some experienced wakeboarders can do 900s. These riders complete two and one-half spins.

Grabs

The grab is another basic wakeboarding trick. As riders jump, they grab a part of the board.

Riders use the front hand for some grabs. To do a method grab, riders grab the heelside edge of the board with the front hand. If they grab the toeside edge, the trick is called a mute grab.

Riders do other grabs with the back hand. During an indy grab, the rider grabs the board's toeside edge with the back hand. If the rider grabs the heelside edge, the trick is called a roast beef.

Extreme Wakeboarding Slang

bonk—to run into an object in the water on purpose

digger—a fall

dock start—a wakeboarding session that begins with the rider standing or sitting on the dock instead of in the water

double-up—a large wake formed when a boat turns around and crosses over its own wake

kicker—a curved ramp

load the line—to pull the rope tight while cutting into the wake

tweak—an extra twist of the body or board added to a trick

wakeskate—a wakeboard with no bindings

Handle passes make tricks more difficult.

Learn about:

- **Tantrums and raleys**
- **Combination tricks**
- **The 1080**

Chapter Three

Extreme Tricks

Many expert wakeboarding tricks are more difficult forms of basic moves. Extreme tricks often include two or more basic moves.

Trick Variations

Riders can make any trick more difficult by doing it fakie or switchstance. To perform a trick fakie, riders do the trick backward or opposite of usual. Riders who do a trick switchstance change their foot position to the opposite of what is normal for them.

Riders also add handle passes to their tricks to make them more difficult. To do a handle pass, the rider moves the handle from one hand to the other while in the air.

After a tantrum, the rider's back faces the wake.

Tantrums and Raleys

A tantrum is like a backward flip. At the beginning of a tantrum, the rider's back is to the wake. The board cuts toward the wake. As the board pops in the air, the rider's head is thrown back. The wake then pushes the rider's feet over the head. Upon landing, the rider's back is again to the wake.

To do a raley, a rider cuts in the wake heelside. As the rider hits the wake, the rider stretches out both arms and legs in the air. The rider looks like the comic book character Superman in flight.

During a raley, the rider looks like Superman.

Combination Tricks

Some of the most extreme tricks are combinations of two or more tricks. Even the best riders must practice a great deal to learn these tricks.

The whirlybird is a tantrum combined with a 360 spin. Riders begin by cutting in the wake as they would do for a tantrum. They turn slightly as they reach the top of the wake. They then throw their arm, shoulder, and head away from the boat.

The whirlybird begins with a tantrum.

This action allows the rider to spin a full circle before landing.

The Pete Rose is another popular combination trick. It combines a toeside roll, a flip, and a handle pass.

The Pete Rose includes a handle pass.

The 1080

Wakeboarders want to keep their sport exciting. The best riders try to invent new tricks and make existing tricks more extreme.

In 2000, rider Parks Bonifay was in Orlando, Florida. Photographers were taking pictures of his tricks. During the photo session, Bonifay became the first rider to complete a 1080. Bonifay spun three full circles in the air. Bonifay's 1080 remains one of the most extreme wakeboarding tricks ever performed.

Parks Bonifay has been a top rider since the 1990s.

All riders should be able to swim well.

Learn about:

Safe places to wakeboard

Safety equipment

Wakeboarding groups

Chapter Four

Safety

Wakeboarding is an exciting sport, but it can be dangerous. Both riders and boat drivers need to follow safety rules.

Wakeboarders should be able to swim well. Even experienced wakeboarders sometimes fall off their boards.

Safe Wakeboarding Places

Wakeboarders should only ride in safe places. Beginners usually start on a calm lake. Only experienced riders can safely ride on water with big waves. Riders should stay away from areas with objects in the water. Logs and rocks can cause injuries. Riders also should stay away from areas crowded with other boats.

Equipment

Riders should check their equipment before each ride. They should make sure the boat is running properly.

Riders should also check their ropes and handles. Wakeboarders need a rope that pulls tight in order to do tricks. The rope must not be worn or frayed. The handle should not have any chips or cracks that could hurt the rider's hands.

Safety Gear

Safe wakeboarders always wear life vests. Waves can overcome even strong swimmers. Life vests can keep riders afloat until they are rescued. Life vests also help protect riders who hit the board, the water, or a ramp. Riders should wear life vests that have been approved by the U.S. Coast Guard.

Wakeboarders sometimes wear wet suits. These waterproof suits keep riders warm in cold water.

Some wakeboarding competitions require riders to wear helmets. Helmets protect the rider's head during jumps and aerial tricks.

Wakeboarding Groups

Several groups organize wakeboarding events. The groups also teach riders about safety.

In 1989, rider Jimmy Redmon formed the World Wakeboard Association (WWA). This group sets competition and safety rules. Other groups that sponsor wakeboarding events are the American Wakeboard Association (AWA), USA Water Ski, Water Ski Canada, and the International Water Ski Federation (IWSF).

Some competitions require riders to wear helmets.

Words to Know

aerial (AIR-ee-uhl)—a trick performed in the air

bindings (BINE-dingz)—the shoelike parts that hold the rider's feet to the board

fakie (FAY-kee)—to perform a trick backward or opposite of the usual position

professional (pruh-FESH-uh-nuhl)—a person who receives money for taking part in a sport

slider (SLY-duhr)—a floating structure of railings used for performing tricks; sliders often are made of plastic pipes.

switchstance (SWICH-stanss)—to perform a trick with the feet in a position opposite of normal; regular-foot riders would stand goofy foot to do a trick switchstance.

wake (WAYK)—a V-shaped set of waves that travels behind a moving boat

To Learn More

Blomquist, Christopher. *Wakeboarding in the X Games.*
A Kid's Guide to the X Games. New York: PowerKids
Press, 2003.

Eck, Kristin. *Wakeboarding: Check it Out!* New York:
Reading Power. PowerKids Press, 2001.

Hayhurst, Chris. *Wakeboarding!: Throw a Tantrum.* The
Extreme Sports Collection. New York: Rosen, 2000.

Useful Addresses

USA Water Ski
1251 Holy Cow Road
Polk City, FL 33868

Water Ski Canada
304-2197 Riverside Drive
Ottawa, ON K1H 7X3
Canada

World Wakeboard Association
P.O. Box 1964
Auburndale, FL 33823

Internet Sites

Track down many sites about extreme wakeboarding.
Visit the FACT HOUND at *http://www.facthound.com*

IT IS EASY! IT IS FUN!

1) Go to *http://www.facthound.com*
2) Type in: 0736815155
3) Click on "FETCH IT" and FACT HOUND will find
   several links hand-picked by our editors.

Relax and let our pal FACT HOUND do the research for you!

Index